The Best Ideas From The Democratic Party

OVER THE PAST 100 YEARS

WITH A FOREWORD FROM
THIS GENERATION'S
FINEST LIBERAL MINDS

Intentionally left blank

Intentionally left blank

4

Intentionally left blank

Intentionally left blank

Intentionally left blank

Intentionally left blank

Intentionally left blank

Intentionally left blank

Intentionally left blank

Intentionally left blank

Intentionally left blank

Intentionally left blank

Intentionally left blank

Intentionally left blank

Intentionally left blank

Intentionally left blank

Intentionally left blank

Intentionally left blank

Intentionally left blank

Intentionally left blank

Intentionally left blank

23

Intentionally left blank

Intentionally left blank

Intentionally left blank

Intentionally left blank

Intentionally left blank

28

Intentionally left blank

Intentionally left blank

Intentionally left blank

Intentionally left blank

Intentionally left blank

33

Intentionally left blank

Intentionally left blank

Intentionally left blank

Intentionally left blank

Intentionally left blank

Intentionally left blank

Intentionally left blank

Intentionally left blank

Intentionally left blank

Intentionally left blank

Intentionally left blank

Intentionally left blank

Intentionally left blank

Intentionally left blank

Intentionally left blank

Intentionally left blank

Intentionally left blank

Intentionally left blank

Intentionally left blank

Intentionally left blank

Intentionally left blank

Intentionally left blank

Intentionally left blank

Intentionally left blank

Intentionally left blank

Intentionally left blank

Intentionally left blank

Intentionally left blank

Intentionally left blank

Intentionally left blank

Intentionally left blank

Intentionally left blank

Intentionally left blank

Intentionally left blank

Intentionally left blank

Intentionally left blank

Intentionally left blank

Intentionally left blank

Intentionally left blank

Intentionally left blank

Intentionally left blank

Intentionally left blank

Intentionally left blank

Intentionally left blank

Intentionally left blank

Intentionally left blank

Intentionally left blank

Intentionally left blank

Intentionally left blank

Intentionally left blank

Intentionally left blank

Intentionally left blank

Intentionally left blank

Intentionally left blank

Intentionally left blank

Intentionally left blank

Intentionally left blank

Intentionally left blank

Intentionally left blank

Intentionally left blank

Intentionally left blank

Intentionally left blank

Intentionally left blank

Intentionally left blank

Intentionally left blank

Intentionally left blank

Intentionally left blank

Intentionally left blank

101

Intentionally left blank

Intentionally left blank

Intentionally left blank

Intentionally left blank

Intentionally left blank

Intentionally left blank

Intentionally left blank

Intentionally left blank

Intentionally left blank

Intentionally left blank

Intentionally left blank

Intentionally left blank

Intentionally left blank

Intentionally left blank

Intentionally left blank

Intentionally left blank

Intentionally left blank

Intentionally left blank

Intentionally left blank

Intentionally left blank

Intentionally left blank

Intentionally left blank

123

Intentionally left blank

Intentionally left blank

Intentionally left blank

Intentionally left blank

Intentionally left blank

Intentionally left blank

Intentionally left blank

Intentionally left blank

131

Find More Books At:
laughoutloudbooks.com

@LOLBooks99

Facebook.com/LOLBooks99

Made in the USA
Middletown, DE
12 March 2015